SRI LANKA
❖
The Emerald Island

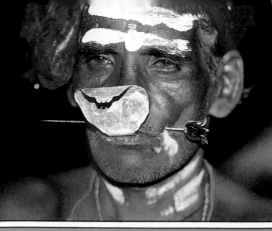

ISBN: 81-7437-66-8

Published by
© **Lustre Press Pvt. Ltd., 1996**
M 75 Greater Kailash II Market
New Delhi 110 048, INDIA
Tel.: (011) 6442271, 6462782, 6460886-0887
Fax: (011) 6467185

Conceived and designed by
Pramod Kapoor at Roli CAD Centre

Printed and bound at
Star Standard Industries Pte. Ltd., Singapore

SRI LANKA

❖

The Emerald Island

Photographs:
DEVIKA GUNASENA

Text:
TISSA DEVENDRA

Lustre Press
·
Roli Books

Foreword

———— ✳ ————

I do not know how many times I've been asked, "Why do you live in Sri Lanka?" This book should save me a good many thousand words of explanation, as it gives an excellent idea of the island's extraordinary appeal. And it was, incidentally, a long book of photographs—Lionel Wendt's classic *Ceylon*—which was my very first introduction to the island years before I actually visited it.

It may well be that each of Sri Lanka's attractions is surpassed somewhere on Earth; Cambodia may have more impressive ruins, Tahiti lovelier beaches, Bali more beautiful landscapes (though I doubt it), Thailand more charming people (ditto). But I find it hard to believe that there is any country which scores so highly in all departments—which has so many advantages, and so few disadvantages, especially for the Western visitor.

Sri Lanka is also the right size, you can drive from one coast to the other in half a day, over roads which are usually good and often excellent, though sometimes afflicted with unusual hazards, such as elephants without rear-lights. Yet despite the fact that the island is only 140 miles across at its widest, it has two distinct climates. The central mountains (up to 7,000 feet high) trap the monsoon rains alternately on the west and the east; unless you are very unlucky; you can always find good weather somewhere in Sri Lanka. And as the island is only a few degrees north of the Equator, winter never comes; however, I once encountered slight ground frost—at midnight, on Christmas Eve, a mile up on the mountains . . .

With a population of some 18,000,000 and an area of 25,000 square miles (just half the size of England), Sri Lanka is not yet too overcrowded and is mercifully spared the appalling poverty and destitution of its giant neighbour. Whether it can continue to avoid India's problems will depend partly on good luck and on its ability to replace politicians with technicians; like all developing countries, it has too many of the former and not enough of the latter. Not the least of the island's fascinations is that it provides a small-scale test case of a multiracial society in transition; the result is often an incongruous and delightful mixture of old and new—like starting the cameras rolling for a movie, or switching on an electronic computer at the auspicious time decreed by the local astrologers.

Though it is probably far too late—for if you have read thus far you may already be doomed—my conscience will not allow me to close without a warning. I came to Sri Lanka in 1956, intending to stay for six months and to write one book about the exploration of the island's coastal waters. Almost thirty years and eighty books later, I am still here, and hope to remain here for the rest of my life. In *The Treasure of the Great Reef* I attempted to analyse this situation, and since I do not think I can improve on the words I wrote then, I take the liberty of quoting a couple of paragraphs from that book.

"Though I never left England until I was thirty-three years old (or travelled more than a score of miles from my birthplace until I was twenty), it is Sri Lanka, not England, that now seems home. I do not pretend to account for this, or for the fact that no other place is wholly real to me. Though London, Washington, New York, Los Angeles, are exciting, amusing, invigorating, and hold all the things that interest my mind, they are no longer quite convincing. Their images are blurred around the edges; like a mirage, they will not stand up to detailed inspection. When I am in the Strand, or 42nd Street, or NASA Headquarters, or the Beverly Hills Hotel, surroundings are liable to give a sudden tremor, and I see through the insubstantial fabric to the reality beneath.

"And always it is the same; the slender palm trees leaning over the white sand, the warm sun sparkling on the waves as they break on the inshore reef, the outrigger fishing boats drawn up high on the beach. This alone is real; the rest is but a dream from which I shall presently awake."

Arthur C. Clarke

5

CONTENTS
✳

Preceding pages 6-7: A Sinhala beauty.

Pages 8-9: Fishermen—these fishermen standing on stilts fishing in shallow waters can be seen in many areas along the coast. They spend hours in the sun and rain, patiently waiting for a catch, precariously perched on their narrow stilts.

Pages 10-11: Brilliance in Piety. Wooden structures brilliantly illuminated depicting the life of the Buddha erected for the Vesak festival which coincides with the full moon day of May.

Pages 12-13: The Fleet is in. Fishing craft jostle in the little harbour of Beruwala—a leading fishing area in the south.

Pages 14-15: *Kings on a Bike. Bunches of king coconuts delicately balanced on a bike enroute to market in Galle.*

Following pages 16-17: *Puppets on Strings. Traditionally costumed puppets for age-old folk dramas are also made by the Ambalangoda mask makers.*

Pages 18-19: *Dances at a Pageant.*

Pages 20-21: *Tender Faith. A pilgrim's offering of naively appliqued lotuses at the Buddha's feet.*

The Land and its People

———————— * ————————

From the seas emerge the green and lovely island of Sri Lanka, its crystalline eastern beaches lapped by the Bay of Bengal, the golden sands, coral reefs and harbours of its western coast facing the sweeping expanse of the Indian Ocean across which sailed, for many thousands of years, traders, travellers, conquerors and missionaries from the four corners of the world to this land they variously called Taprobane, Serendib or Ceylon. Thousands of miles of sea ebb and flow between Sri Lanka's southernmost point and the next landfall, Antarctica's icy waste. Its northern peninsula and scattered islets stretch but a few short miles, across the shallow Palk Strait, from the southern cape of India—a route travelled, since time began, by settlers, traders, envoys, missionaries, invaders, smugglers and now terrorists. Its physical separation from its giant neighbour, however, has endowed Sri Lanka with a distinct cultural and political identity for over 3,000 years.

It is incredibly beautiful, this last remnant of a great prehistoric continent now sunk in the deep ocean. Sri Lanka's uniqueness causes the beholder flying across the arid brown wastes of the south Indian plain to be startled by the dramatic contrast of this lush green island with its granite peaks —a glistening gem set in an indigo-blue sea. Sri Lankans boast that their sea-grit little island, of 25,000 square miles, contains every variety of landscape other than snowy mountains. This is largely true. The topography of the island slopes gradually upwards from its beaches, to plains of paddy fields, coconuts and dense forests, through mountain valleys and slopes thickly carpetted with tea and rubber plantations to cloud-topped mountain peaks set in a temperate landscape of rhododendron, fir and pine. Tumbling streams cascade in waterfalls and rapids to become sedate rivers nourishing rice fields before they flow into the sea. The beaches are paradisal— huge stretches in the east where forest and mangrove abut the fringing coconut palms, or the smaller bays and coral reefs of the south-west coast. Over the centuries, man has shaped this land and the land, in turn, has moulded the visions and way of life of its peoples.

In the dim dawn of prehistory, stone-age man probably trekked to Sri Lanka across the shallow waters and sand bars that linked it to the sub-continental mainland. They followed the path trodden by the prey they hunted—deer, wild boar, elephant and an immense variety of

Facing page: Under Sail. An ontrigger boat, of age-old design sets out to sea.

23

wildfowl. Archaeological excavations, over the past few decades, have unearthed a far greater spread of stone-age habitations than had ever been imagined. Settlements and artifacts have been unearthed in Yala in the south-east coast, urn burials of great antiquity have been found in the ancient harbour of Mantai in the north west, cave dwellings have been explored in the central hills and the impressive tomb of a stone age chief, built of immense granite slabs, reminiscent of Stonehenge, stands amidst the foothills of Padavigampola, forty miles inland, an awe inspiring monument to the first man in Sri Lanka. Stone age man in Sri Lanka slipped back into the mists of prehistory as mysteriously as he had emerged from them leaving behind a thousand conundrums for archaeologists to uncover.

Centuries later, along the same land route, now lost, came the Veddah tribes of Australoid hunters. They have stayed on, to earn the distinction of being the islands's oldest people. The vast forests that carpetted Sri Lanka were a rich hunting ground for the Veddah clans. They lived in small groups in caves, or lean-tos of branches, and never built houses or cultivated land. Their life was in close harmony with the wilderness that sustained them. Their rituals of homage to their forest deities have been preserved, amazingly unchanged, from the dim past to the present day, providing a rich resource for modern anthropologists. When the ancestors of the Sinhalese arrived in Sri Lanka, the Veddahs made a conscious choice not to join the mainstream of civilization but to retain their age-old way of life. They withdrew deeper into their native wilderness which sustained them. They hunted game with bow and arrow and simple traps; they dug for edible yams, picked fruit, outwitted bears to gather wild honey, and clothed themselves in leaves and animal skins. They honoured their forest gods with rituals of dance and trance. It was deliberate choice and not armed conflict that made them so distance themselves from the civilization of settled villages and the newcomers, since these were so incredibly different from their own simple nomadic life in the great forest which they never harmed. However, they lived in harmony with their settled neighbours, bartering forest produce for metal knives, arrow heads and such implements. On religious and festive occasions of the Sinhalese, the Veddah chieftains participated to make obeisance, pay ritual tributes and perform their hunter's dances. Amazingly, this two thousand year old tradition is yet maintained when the Veddahs emerge from their forest to dance at the annual procession of the Mahiyangana temple, built on the age-old border between the Sinhala settlements and Veddah country. The push of an expanding population is now depleting the forest and expanding cultivation. The pull of the amenities and attractions of modern "civilization" has proved far more difficult to resist than the gentle agrarian life of the ancient Sinhalese from which the Veddahs had withdrawn earlier. Today they are a sadly depleted people, struggling to maintain their unique identity against the almost irresistible forces of assimilation and modernity. It will be a tragic day for Sri Lanka if and when its first people cease to be.

Three thousand or so years ago, the first settlers from the Indo-Aryan peoples of the sub-continent sailed to Sri Lanka and established permanent settlements, mainly in the north-west and south-west of the country. They were not casual travellers or shipwrecked sailors, but participants in a planned pattern of settlement in a virgin land whose resources would have been observed by navigators and traders. These new settlers were from the settled civilization of the Indo-Ganges plain, who conducted expeditions in search of colonisation, sailing here in large ships. They would have arrived with language, religious beliefs, agricultural practices and a way of life which, over the centuries, gradually evolved into a distinct culture as links with the Indian homeland quietly dissolved. These new settlers called themselves the Sinhalese-the Lion Race. Sinhala tradition traces their origins to Vijaya, an adventurous prince who sailed from Bengal in north-east India to settle with his entourage in north-west Sri Lanka. This great adventure has long been sprinkled with the gilt of legend and fantasy. Vijaya's sailors were lured, they say, by Kuveni — a sorceress-queen of astounding beauty who transformed them into animals. Brave Vijaya defeated Kuveni, rescued his men, and took her for his consort. He used her infatuation to defeat her own people, only to abandon her later to be killed by her former subjects. Vijaya then married a princess from India and established the first dynasty from which all Sinhala kings claim descent. The patina of legend gliding the kernel of truth clearly symbolizes the triumph of the Vijayan settlers over the earlier settlements and the establishment of one royal lineage and one unified kingdom. Anuradhapura, in the Central plains, was the royal capital of the Sinhala kingdom for over a thousand years.

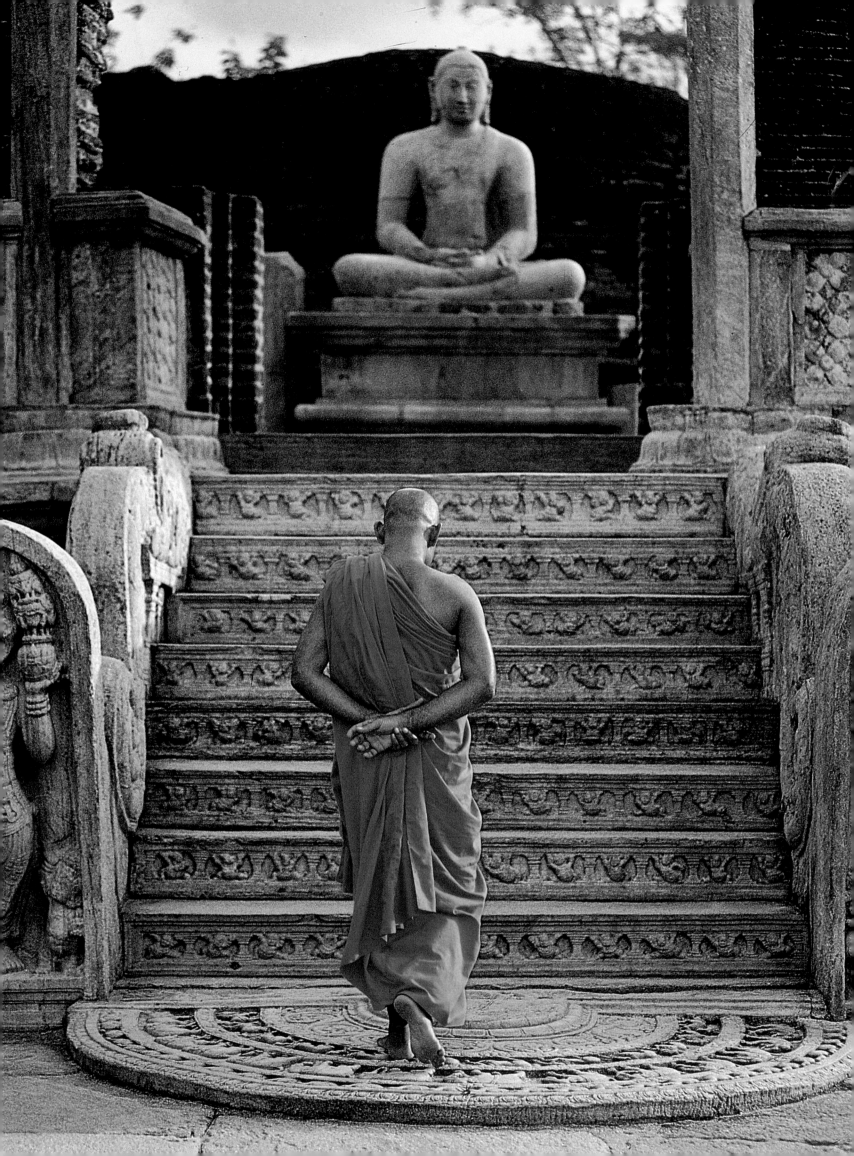

Religion and Culture

———— * ————

The defining event in Sinhala civilization was its adoption of Buddhism 2,300 years ago. India's great emperor Ashoka sent his son, the venerable Mahinda, as a missionary of Buddhism to Devanampiya Tissa, the Sinhala King of Anuradhapura. The ancient chronicles record this mission as an unprecedented phenomenon where, not only were the King and his nobles convinced of the eternal truth of Buddhism, but also the entire populace adopted the new creed. Searching for an explanation, from today's perspective, it is probable that the simple agrarian civilization that had developed in Sri Lanka, far distanced from its Indian origins, neither imported nor developed a Brahminical or priestly caste or a formalized religion. Spiritual needs would have been fulfilled by simple deities of hearth and home, crafts, farm and forest and the all-powerful elements. It is an intriguing possibility that the pre-Buddhist Sinhalese paid great homage to trees, with which they have always shown great affinity. Most Sinhala names of villages and towns are derived from trees and even today, individual allotments or houses are described by the trees that flourish on them and are thus recorded in title deeds. In consonance with this indigenous tradition, Mahinda's mission was followed by that of his sister, the nun Sanghamitta, who brought King Tissa the priceless gift of a sapling of the great Bodhi tree beneath which the Buddha attained enlightenment in Gaya. The tree, sanctified by the doctrine that the Buddha preached beneath its boughs is yet alive and has been venerated in Anuradhapura for 2,300 years by Sinhala Buddhists long after its parent withered away in India. Sinhala Buddhists, therefore, are convinced that the link between the people and Buddhism is a sacred and indissoluble trust which defines their identity and has withstood the vicissitudes of history and hostile invaders over the ages.

Buddhism inspired a cultural revolution and an architectural flowering in Anuradhapura which transformed the capital into one of the wonders of the region. Kings vied with each other to build gigantic stupas, monumental Buddha statues, beautifully landscaped monasteries and massive palaces. The many storied Brazen Palace was roofed with gleaming tiles of copper. Extensive monastery environs were laid out with complex water gardens where stone lined channels gently led water to fountains and elaborately carved ponds. Many monasteries were cooled

Facing page: Meditation at the Circular Relic Chamber, Polonnaruwa. A Buddhist monk bows in meditation before a granite seated Buddha at the Circular Relic Chamber. He stands on an exquisitely ornamented moonstone which leads on to the carved granite stairway to the temple.

by a fascinating system of channels that guided a stream of water into a surrounding moat and in between to cool the building. These buildings were also equipped with delightfully carved toilets yet to be seen, along with an amazingly efficient system of sewage disposal by water. Such monasteries were spread throughout the length and breadth of the island and impress the modern observer with the piety that made so many thousands take to the monastic life of the Buddhist Sangha.

A unique feature of Anuradhapura's Buddhist architecture are the enormous stupas of brick and mortar which enclosed elaborate chambers enshrining relics of the Buddha. These man-made mountains dominate the landscape even now and would have been amazingly impressive with their gleaming plaster domes crowned with glistening pinnacles.

Two great religious establishments, Maha Vihara and Abhayagiri,

The Golden Temple-The Ruwanveli Seya (stupa of golden sand) is the most famous in Sinhala chronicles, as it was built by the great hero King Dutugemunu in 250 B.C. It has since been restored and is viewed standing majestically in the ancient city of Anuradhapura.

dominated the spiritual life of the capital and attracted scholars from all over the Buddhist world. The famous Buddhist pilgrims Fa Hien and Huen Tsang spent years here and carried back with them many Buddhist sacred texts and wisdom gained from these seats of learning.

The Anuradhapura kingdom was never parochial and inward-looking. It traded and had relations with many countries. Kosmas the ancient writer wrote, 'As its position is central, the island is a great resort of ships, from all parts of India, and from Persia and Ethiopia, and in like manner it despatches many of its own to foreign ports'. Foreigners lived and traded in this country whose main port was Mantai (Mannar) for many centuries. Much evidence has recently been uncovered of items originating from China, Arabia, Greece, Rome and other countries establishing its central position in, what is now described as, the maritime silk road between Europe, Africa, West Asia and the Far East. Sri Lanka's maritime history is only now being compiled from underwater explorations, reinterpreted inscriptions and ancient chronicles of other countries. It is clear, however, that the country had a vibrant maritime tradition with large ships that sailed to the Far East and South East Asia trading in fine textiles, gems, rare woods and ivory. Rome, Cairo and Peking record embassies from Sri Lanka's kings. Indonesia, Burma, Thailand, Laos, Cambodia and China welcomed missionaries and envoys from Sri Lanka who made a great impact on the development of Buddhism in these lands. Legendary travellers of yore, Ibn Batuta and Marco Polo too, visited Sri Lanka a few centuries later, when the kingdom was on the decline.

Ancient waters, Guardian trees. Huge old trees growing on the edge of an ancient reservoir in Anuradhapura, Sri Lanka's first capital for a thousand years.

The economic foundation of the ancient kingdom was constituted by its mastery of hydraulic engineering which enabled the cultivation of enormous extents of rice fields in the central plains. Rivers and streams flowing down from the central hills were impounded with enormous dams to create huge reservoirs, as large as small harbours. A finely engineered system of canals led water into smaller reservoirs and then on to the rice fields below them. The capital of Anuradhapura received all its water, both for consumption and the elaborate monastery water gardens, from a reservoir almost 40 miles away—an engineering feat unparalleled in South Asia. These enormous works were constructed by a well developed system of service tenure—where every village despatched a self-sufficient team of workers to construct and repair national irrigation systems for a specific period. There was no slavery or wage labour.

The ancient kingdom never had a standing army. Here again each village contributed a squad of self-provisioned militia to the royal army whenever called upon. The professional soldiery were invariably mercenaries hired from India to serve under the king's generals.

War was an ever present danger. The rich pickings possible from this prosperous kingdom served as a magnet for invaders and freebooters from south India, a few short miles across the narrow straits. However, no invader ever occupied the whole island. They were content to rule the rich central kingdom of Anuradhapura, while the rightful rulers fled to the southern principality of Ruhuna. Here they rebuilt their forces till they were strong enough to strike back and reclaim their throne. Two

Paws of the Great Lion. These enormous and beautifully carved lion's paws frame the ceremonial stairway to the King Kasyapa's royal palace on Sigiriya, the Lion Rock (5th century).

great heroes, separated by a thousand years, tower in Sri Lanka's history. Dutugemunu in 250 B.C. and Vijayabahu in 1100 A.D. both emerged from their redoubts in Ruhuna to expel the invaders and recapture the throne of Anuradhapura.

In the 6th century A.D. emerged perhaps the most fascinating king in Sri Lanka's history — Kasyapa—who usurped his father's throne, gave up Anuradhapura and built a completely new capital city on the towering rock of Sigiriya about sixty miles south of the old capital. His initial move would have been strategic, as Sigiriya, the Lion Rock, dominates the plains and is superbly defensible, but Kasyapa was, above all, a lover of beauty. He distanced himself from the asceticism of Buddhism and exhorted his artists and engineers to build a magnificent palace in the sky—the likes of which have never been equalled. A magnificent complex of palaces, assembly halls, 'hanging gardens' and water gardens enfold the precipitous rock and its environs. They yet amaze us 1,500 years later. Shallow caves in the rock painted with frescoes of lovely maidens show an artistic genius whose heights were never again reached. Their colours yet glow with the beauty they depict. Kasyapa's brilliant but brief reign ended in his defeat and death. Anuradhapura reclaimed its rightful place and the hedonistic Xanadu of Sigiriya became a monastery.

Recent studies have moved the focus of technological achievements from the superbly complex irrigation network to other fields. The engineering skills that moved enormous stone beams to shore up many storied monastries and Sigiriya's ethereal palaces were clearly based on

Cloud Princesses. Two of the incomparably beautiful maidens painted 1,500 years ago on the rocky walls of the mountain palace of Sigiriya, the Lion Rock.

a recorded corpus of scientific learning. This equally applied to the management of the huge resources of manpower to construct reservoirs, aquaducts and stupas. Granite is the hardest of stones, but Sri Lanka's sculptors and builders used it with the same panache and artistry that Greeks and Romans brought to soft marble. The gentle contemplative smile of the 2,000 year old Buddha images has been wrested out of unyielding granite.

Following pages 32-33: *Meditation in Stone. This perfectly preserved granite eighth century Buddha sits in perennial meditation within an elaborate arch under the parasol of royalty, carved in relief on the roof of the man-made granite cave and attended to by divine beings holding* Chamara *(yak-hair whisks). This temple is today called the Gal Vihara Temple of Granite.*

It is also possible that the images of the Buddha sculpted in Sri Lanka were the first in the world. Recent discoveries in south-east Sri Lanka solved the puzzle of this mastery over stone. An elaborate system of smelting furnaces using the force of monsoon winds has been discovered, capable of producing steel of the highest quality. This is the legendary steel of Damascene that, as the Arabs believe, came from Serendib. Chinese chronicles record many-decked ships from Sri Lanka, arriving with valuable cargo and exquisite muslins woven in that country. Pearls which abounded in the banks off Mannar and gems in the central hills were crafted into elaborate jewelery for royalty and export. Buddha statues and images of deities cast in bronze and precious metals show exquisite workmanship. No written records, unfortunately, record these skills and technology. The artifacts only stand as silent proof.

At the Master's Feet. A young acolyte pays homage at the feet of the granite statue of the Buddha in Parinibbana at Polonnaruwa's Gal Vihara (Temple of Granite).

Sri Lanka has the proud distinction of having a continuous written record of its history from the pre-Christian era to the fall of the last independent kingdom in 1815. This is the Mahavansa, the Great Chronicle, where monks recorded on palm leaf manuscripts the rise and fall of Sinhala rulers and their kingdoms. This continuous record, unique in world history, has been proved accurate by archaeological evidence and, amazingly, has even enabled historians to fix dates in Indian history.

The history of the great Anuradhapura kingdom is as chequered as any. Rival dynasties fought for the throne. Marauding expeditions from south India grew increasingly frequent. The capital was shifted to the

Facing page: *Unchanging Tradition. Young Buddhist monks, before a ruined Buddha of stone at Polonnaruwa (12th century).*

more defensible Polonnaruwa where there was a renaissance of architectural and sculptural splendor, though on a smaller scale and in a more ornate style. The massive group of Buddha sculptures at Gal Vihara awes the beholder with its scale and serenity. The Polonnaruwa kingdom fell to the powerful Chola empire of south India which expanded to encompass even Indonesia. Its hostile army laid to waste towns, monasteries and reservoirs. In time the Cholas were defeated and withdrew leaving behind some settlers in the bleak northern peninsula of Jaffna. The kingdoms that rose after this never attained the grandeur of the Golden Age.

Driven by famine, disease, and fear of Indian marauders, the Sinhala people gradually drifted south-west to the more secure mountains, and lush green valleys where they developed a totally different type of

The Feet of the Master. The delicately carved feet and pleated robe of the massive Buddha statue of brick and plaster, now standing ravaged and headless in the roofless ruin of the Lankatilaka Vihara in Polonnaruwa, the country's second capital (12th century)

civilization—of little village communities, each with their small rice fields and simple domestic interests. These were Sri Lanka's dark ages. The ancient kingdom had been abandoned to the grim jungle, its magnificent monasteries and palaces reduced to vast mounds of lonely ruins. By the 15th century the most powerful of these late kingdoms was established at Kotte, a few miles off the coast, near the future harbour of Colombo. For a brief period this kingdom gave rise to the last great Sinhala civilization. This was, however, the last bright flicker of the flame of Sinhala sovereignty before it was snuffed out.

Facing page: *The Master meditates. The gigantic granite Buddha in meditation, framed by a ceremonial royal arch of the Polonnaruwa period. This is one of the images in the great granite triptych of Polonnaruwa's Gal Vihara.*

Colonial Conquests and
Independence
———— ✳ ————

The Portuguese conquistadores who arrived in Sri Lanka with the dawn of the 16th Century heralded 500 years of European colonial domination and consequent isolation from its Asian neighbours. These adventurers came to displace the Arab traders who controlled the spice trade. But they were not mere traders. They became conquerors who established large plantations of cinnamon for export to Europe. Mere trade was not their aim. They had banished the Arabs from the spice trade and aimed to establish a monopoly and resist all other European interlopers. Political suzerainty was their goal which they established by a shrewd system that inextricably linked sword and Bible. The kingdom of Kotte rapidly declined into a client state, its king and nobility were converted to Catholicism. The last feeble king finally bequeathed his kingdom to the King of Portugal. However, the flame of revolt was kept alive by rebel princes who escaped Portugal's deathly embrace and established the independent kingdoms of Sitawaka and Kandy in the central hills. The maritime provinces and ports were under Portuguese control, largely isolating the interior kingdoms from access to direct foreign trade and allies. Throughout the period of their occupation the Portuguese mounted several expeditions to capture the kingdom of Kandy, but were outwitted by guerilla warfare and the wild mountainous terrain.

The Portuguese made a far greater cultural impact on Sri Lanka than the Dutch and British who succeeded them. Inspite of its association with the invader, Catholicism rapidly gained ground in the maritime provinces, clearly striking a congenial vein. Today, Catholics constitute an active and vital minority, having withstood the persecution of the Dutch and discouragement of the British. The coastal belt, north of Colombo, abounds in Mediterranean styled churches and brightly painted statues of saints, crucifixes and grottoes. The church has been thoroughly indigenised and adapted to the Sinhala way of life. An unusual feature among the Sinhalese has been their ready adoption of Portuguese names. The telephone directory abounds in names such as De Silva, Perera and Fernando. Strangely, most of them are not Catholics, unlike in neighbouring India.

As Portuguese power dwindled in Europe and along the seaways to Asia, they were displaced by the Dutch, who defeated the Portuguese and tightened their hold over the ports and coastline, thus completely

Facing page: *Bygone Glory. An antique bull drawn 'buggy' rests in the large portico of the manorial home of a wealthy family.*

isolating the Kandyan kingdom and hastening its decline into a parochial, inward-looking relic of past glory. The Dutch were methodical in all their activities. They built roads to their cinnamon plantations, instituted a system of land registration and established a system of justice, based on Roman-Dutch law which yet remains the bedrock of Sri Lanka's legal system. Strangely enough the Dutch occupation was not by a national army—it was by the Dutch East Indian Company, the world's first multi-national commercial enterprise. It drew its cadres from all over Europe and its army from mercenary regiments of Luxemburg and Switzerland. When the Dutch surrendered to the British, many of these Europeans stayed back to constitute the Burgher community. This was a small group whose impact on the civil service, legal profession, scholarship and politics of Sri Lanka has been of great significance.

Democracy's First Home. The Greek and Roman building in Colombo where the country's legislatures sat and debated for half a century. It is now the Presidential Secretariat.

The Dutch, defeated by Napoleon in Europe, surrendered to the British in 1796. The impressive fortresses they built in every harbour, which yet awe the beholder with their battlements, all capitulated without firing a shot. The British had no intention of allowing an independent Sinhala kingdom, however powerless, to fester in the heart of its island colony. In 1815 the British employed subversion and sabotage to persuade the nobility of the Kandyan kingdom to depose their monarch and surrender him and their kingdom to the British King. Thus, ingloriously, ended a royal line stretching back to 2,400 years.

Facing page: *A Spanish touch. A Catholic church in the staunchly Catholic suburb of Mutuwal in Colombo, has a facade typical of the Iberian countries that introduced this faith in Sri Lanka.*

The British imposed Pax Britannica and the modern world on its new Crown Colony. Cinnamon declined in importance. Coffee, and later, tea plantations replaced the virgin jungles of the hill country. Rubber and coconut took over village gardens. Roads and railways were pushed into the plantation areas to transport produce speedily to the bustling harbour of Colombo for export to Europe. In characteristically systematic British style, a highly centralised network of colonial administration replaced the traditional system. A graded system of officials and officers radiated down from the capital city of Colombo, to provincial capitals such as Kandy, Galle and Jaffna and thence to every village. This system was paralleled with courts of justice, hospitals, engineering services, land surveys and registration. Apart from primary schools, education was left to the Christian missionaries. All these measures and institutions

Galle, a southern town, has the famous Dutch fort, churches and other old buildings. It has a beautiful natural harbour which was an important gateway to the country in the days gone by. These old buildings show the Dutch influence that prevails in and around this area.

provided the British with an efficiently administered, well-roaded little island and a law abiding people of reasonable education. However, it was difficult to persuade an independent peasantry to work as wage-labour on the huge plantations the British planters had allocated to themselves out of traditional lands. The need was met by the import of tens of thousands of indentured Tamil labourers from south India who were to live for generations incarcerated in sub-human barracks in plantations, isolated from the general populace.

The wheel of history quietly turned. With the end of World War II the sun set on the British Empire and Ceylon gained its independence in

Facing page: *Ramparts. The Dutch Fort which dominates the southern city of Galle is in excellent condition as it surrendered to the British without firing a shot.*

43

1948. Sovereignty was exercised by an elected legislature established several years earlier, when Ceylon was awarded universal suffrage with considerable local autonomy. Since then the country has been a parliamentary democracy with elections held at regular intervals. In 1972 the country officially became a republic. It adopted its ancient name of Sri Lanka and gave up the colonial 'Ceylon'. In 1978 the republic adopted its ancient Executive Presidential system together with an elected Parliament.

Over the years Sri Lanka has developed a widespread network of social welfare. Good health facilities have ensured a population with an extremely low rate of infant mortality and the life expectancy of developed Western countries. Free education at school and university has given Sri Lanka almost universal literacy.

Kovil Guardian. An old man sits on the doorstep of a Kovil in Colombo.

The Sinhalese have a sense of mystical unity with the land of Sri Lanka. To them, this land, and no other, is their one and only home. The aboriginal Veddahs' loyalty is to their immediate locality with no concept of the island entity. The Sinhalese, on the other hand, look back on a long history when their ancient kings ruled the entire land till foreign invaders nibbled away at it till it finally succumbed to the overwhelming power of a modern industrial state. All other peoples who now live in Sri Lanka are seen as late comers whose gut loyalty is to "motherlands" across the sea from which they came - and with which they often share a language, way of life and faith. This sense of unity

Facing page: *Patience and Faith. A 'Kapurala' (lay priest of the old gods) awaits worshippers by the sadly decaying frescoes of the shrine to God Natha at Kandy.*

between the Sinhalese and the land of Sri Lanka has been cemented by the fact that this is the only home of the Sinhala people. They do not share their language or culture with any one of the myriad peoples on the Indian subcontinent, or elsewhere. This makes them a unique people. But this emotion has never degenerated into hostility towards later arrivals in the island - even though some of them are descended from former invaders.

The Sinhalese are the dominant segment of the population - 75% of a population of 18 million, and are widespread throughout the country. A few centuries ago, they abandoned their ancient sites in the northern peninsula on account of its vulnerability to invaders from south India, whose Tamil descendants now occupy this land. Over the centuries the Sinhalese have developed a life style and culture distinct from that of the Indian subcontinent. Their unwavering adherence to Buddhism, after its disappearance in India, has made it, in many ways, closer in its way of life to the Buddhist lands of South East Asia - Burma, Thailand, Cambodia and Laos.

The Tamils are the next largest group of people and they fall into two distinct categories. The first group are those descended from settlers in the north of a few centuries ago. The area they have traditionally occupied has been in the north. Over the years, however, they have moved eastwards along the coastline and now share this area with Muslims and Sinhalese. A perceived sense of discrimination has driven some of these Tamils to take up arms and wage a campaign of terrorism and guerilla warfare against the national government demanding an independent Tamil state. Tamils, however, are found all over the country and are a highly visible presence in the capital city of Colombo and the major towns. They play a significant role in politics, commerce, law, medicine and the civil service.

Distinct from these ancient settlers are the Tamil descendants of the indentured labourers in the plantations who arrived in the country a mere century ago. Most of them yet live in enclaves in and around the plantation areas in the central hill country. Their contribution to the country's plantation economy is immense but their community, though a powerful vote bank, remains distinct and is yet poorly integrated into the life of the wider community. Strangely, the two Tamil communities, almost equal in numbers and sharing the same language, rarely intermingle and guard their individual identities. All Tamils speak the same language of south India and their culture is identical to that of Tamil Nadu.

The Muslims of Sri Lanka, constituting about 7% of its people are almost a text book example of peaceful co-existence. They are descendants of Arab traders and south Indian Muslims whose Islamic identity has kept them distinct, culturally and geographically, from the

Tamils whose language they share. Muslim villages are found in many areas of the country, side by side with Sinhalese and Tamil communities. Many are found in the south-western coastal belt. Others are in the central hills where the King of Kandy gave them refuge from Portuguese conquistadores five centuries ago. These Muslims are, by and large, traders and businessmen ranging from itinerant pedlars to merchant princes. Muslim traders are a vital component in every bazaar and commercial centre. In the East, however, the Muslims are rice-farmers of great productivity cultivating enormous extents of land which constitute the country's rice bowl. Muslims are well integrated into the life of the country and are well represented in all walks of life and are a significant political force.

The Malaya of Sri Lanka are also Muslims but are recognised as a different people. Sailors, traders and even invaders from Malaya and Java have been recorded in the ancient chronicles. The 'modern' Malays are, however, descended from soldiers brought across from Indonesia by the Dutch and political exiles from the same region. Many of them continued to serve the British and, later on, the national armed forces, truc to their fighting traditions. Today they are a community well integrated but separate, loyal to Islam but distinct from their co-religionists. They are proud of their heritage, traditions and distinctive dialect. Malays have distinguished themselves in military careers but are also well represented in the civil services, commerce and the learned professions.

The Burghers of Sri Lanka occupy a unique social niche among other peoples of European descent in Asia. These descendants of European invaders, some of them boasting of centuries-old genealogies, cultivated a way of life which bridged Europe and Asia—with the emphasis on Europe. They proudly kept their family names (such as Brohier, Herft, Sansoni), their Christian faith, western costumes and the English language as a link with their European origins. For most of the British period they dominated the legal and medical professions and the civil services. But many became uneasy with the growing dominance of the national languages after independence. A perceived fear of their Europeanness being swamped inspired many of them to emigrate to Australia. Many stayed back and they yet constitute a small but important group whose distinct character is yet intact. Retention of Burgher identity never meant an exclusive ghetto culture. There have always been intermarriages between Sinhalese and Tamils, often producing a fascinating amalgam of life styles and racial types.

Following pages 48-49: Praise Allah. Colombo's Muslims at a community prayer on the Hadj festival day at Galle Face Green marine esplanade.

Festivals and Celebrations
————————— ✻ —————————

The Theravada Buddhism of Sri Lanka, which it shares with Burma, Thailand, Laos and Cambodia has, over the last 2,300 years developed a uniquely Sinhalese flavour. The chaste and monastic puritanism of the doctrine has been overlaid with a colourful amalgam of practices drawn from folk ritual and Hindu worship. The typical vilage temple is set in a wide sandy garden scrupulously swept by acolytes. A bell shaped stupa dominates the premises, containing relics of the Buddha. The Bo-tree spreads its wide branches over simple altars laden with flowers and clay lamps flickering in the alcoves of the parapet wall. Not far is the Vihara, the image house, with a large Buddha statue in a chamber lined with cool porcelain tiles. The outer chamber is painted with scenes of the Buddha's life and previous incarnations. The doorway is guarded by heavenly giants with drawn swords. Not far from this is a smaller Hindu "devale" (home of gods) redolent of camphor and incense, tributes to the resident deities. After Buddhist devotees pay their respects to the Vihara, Bo-tree and stupa, they move to the devala to make their vows for earthly success and to receive divine blessings from the officiating "Kapurala". On every full moon day every Buddhist temple throbs with the muted hum of prayers and is fragrant with the scent of blossoms heaped on altars by white clad worshippers.

The Poson festival in June is of special significance to Sinhalese Buddhists as it marks the anniversary of their nation's embrace of Buddhism. The centre of the celebration is the ancient capital of Anuradhapura with its myriad temples and sacred sites. Hundreds of thousands of pilgrims pour into the ancient city by road and rail. They camp out in the open and spend their time in meditation and worship at the sacred Bo-tree and numerous hallowed temples and stupas many centuries old. The last full moon day in December is of great meaning to women for it honours the nun Sanghamitta who carried the sacred Bo-sapling to Sri Lanka twenty-three centuries ago. The night is made colourful by processions of women devotees carrying an image of the great woman.

Vesak in May honours the birth of the Buddha. Every temple is crowded with worshippers; towns and villages flutter with streamers and the multi-coloured Buddhist flag. On the great night towns and cities

Facing page: *An old dancer performing the torch-dance.*
Following pages 52-53: *The scenic Seemamalaka, brightly illuminated on Vesak full moon day, is situated on the waters of the Peira lake. It is part of the Gangarama temple, Colombo. This above of peace, away from the busy thoroughfares is used for meditation, prayers and other religious activities. The lake was originally built by Dutch, connecting a number of canals which were earlier used for the transportation of goods.*

become fairylands of light and colour. Every Buddhist home is decorated with colourful lanterns and twinkling lights. Every prominent building and plaza blazes with that unique phenomenon - the Vesak pandal. These are huge facades of canvas and bamboo scaffolding covered with paintings of Buddhist stories. What is unusual is the unimaginably intricate swirling patterns of electric illumination before which gather goggle-eyed crowds of spectators, while music plays and loudspeakers blare out the stories depicted. Colombo is especially rich in these pandals and city streets are clogged with visitors from afar, crowded in buses and trucks, mixing worship with night-seeing.

In August, Kandy is the centre of celebration when its streets are paraded for a week by the magnificent processions of the Esala Parabhera. This glorious parade of manificently costumed elephants,

Songs of Praise. Bands of singers parade the city on Vesak night, singing devotional songs on Buddhist themes celebrating the Buddha's birth.

dancers and chieftains dates from the days of the kings of Kandy. Over a hundred elephants move slowly along in stately order, caparisoned in crimson and gold, blue and silver. Huge tuskers carry relic caskets of silver and gold. Troupes of superbly costumed dancers leap and cavort in age-old movements to the pulsating rhythms of teams of drummers. Sidewalks, shops and houses are tightly packed with crowds to watch this glorious spectacle. It honours the Sacred Relic of the Buddha's

Facing page: A colourful array of lighted candles at St. Anthony's church, Kochchikade. People of all religions come here on Tuesday to pray to this loving saint to solve their problems and to fulfil their vows for favours granted.
Following pages 56-57: An old dancer, performing in the southern tradition, makes rings of fire with his torch in a temple procession.

Tooth enshrined in Kandy's royal temple of the Dalada Maligawa, and inextricably linked in tradition with Sinhala sovereignty.

In April comes the great spectacular celebration of the Sinhala New Year which dawns on the 13th of the month. Shops and work places close down for a week, after a hectic splurge of buying clothes and gifts for the festival. Everybody travels back to their village homes where families gather round their elders. The great day dawns at the auspicious hour decreed by astrologers, to the sound of fire crackers and drums. Homage is paid to elders and families sit down to a traditional feast dressed in bright new clothes of the year's lucky colour chosen by astrologers. The season is devoted to merry making, folk games and visiting kinsfolk.

The year's first quarter is the season of pilgrimage to Sri Pada, also

Dance of Devotion. A Tamil woman, head shaved in penance, dances in a trance before the shrine of the God Skanda at Kataragama.

known as Adam's Peak, the impressive 7,000 foot mountain dominating the southern central hills. A gigantic footprint carved on the rock's highest point has been the object of wonder and worship from time immemorial. Legend has it that the Buddha left this footprint while on a celestial journey. A Buddhist temple has crowned the summit for many centuries and draws an unending stream of pilgrims, chanting devotional songs as they climb the chilly and precipitous slopes in family groups. This exhausting pilgrimage is a deeply moving experience. Hindu worshippers too perform this pilgrimage, convinced it is a footprint of the God Shiva. Buddhists and Hindus worship here side by side in harmony as they share the heart-stopping drama of sunrise from Sri Pada.

Over the last five centuries, Sinhala Catholics have developed their indigenous style of honouring their faiths. Saints' days are celebrated with verve and vitality in the large plazas before the ornate facades of churches. Colourful fiestas and fairs are held under the huge flagstaff of pennants and flags which flutter throughout the festival's duration. Certain old churches in various parts of the country have developed into places of popular pilgrimage for Catholics.

Most rural Catholics of the coastal belt are fisher folk and one of their most colourful celebrations is held in the lagoons and harbours just north of Colombo where a fleet of gaily bedecked fishing boats sail along to be blessed by their priests and honour the Virgin Mary. The most moving Catholic celebration is the Passion Play of the fishing village of Duwa. As in the internationally famous Oberammengau, the traditional

The Rhythm of Drums. The lively beat of a variety of drums accompanying the dancers of the Navam Maha Perahera procession.

roles of Christ's passion are played by simple village men and women in the open air. A devout audience follows the age-old drama enacted in sonorous Sinhalese and are immensely moved by this sacred spectacle.

In many ways Sri Lanka's most eclectic religious festival takes place in July in Kataragama in the southern coast. Not so very long ago this was a shrine in the jungle on the outskirts of the Yala National Park. Today its immense popularity has made it a bustling, though pilgrim-oriented town. It is the shrine of the Hindu god Skanda honoured by Hindus but simultaneously identified as Kataragama Deviyo, a guardian deity of the Sinhala nation. He is endowed with the genius to grant boons and favours. This reputation draws pilgrims in thousands who line up to pray for success and, in turn, offer valuable gifts to the god. His worship is largely Hindu

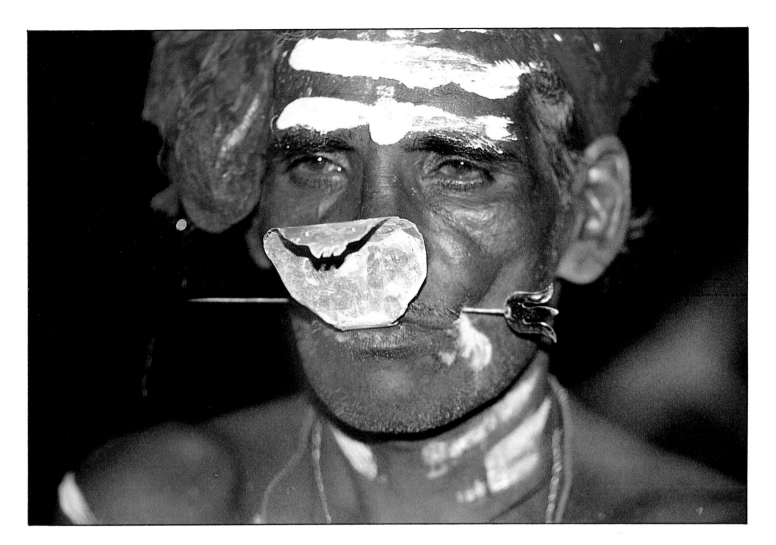

in ritual and the annual festival is a fascinating display of penitents dancing in a trance, hanging from hooks and most famously, fire-walking.

The Hindu festivals of Sri Lanka are identical to those of Tamil Nadu from where they originated. The harvest festival of Thai Pongal; Deepavali celebrating the victory of light over darkness are observed in Tamil areas and Hindu homes with the traditional rituals of south India. Hindu Kovils with their colourful, ornate gopurams are found in many towns and they often have a chariot festival where the elaborately carved carriage of the god is drawn in procession through the streets to the ancient rhythms of Carnatic music.

Islam is the most austere of the faiths in Sri Lanka and does not go in for the colourful processions of Buddhists and Hindus. The most visible Muslim celebration is the feast of Id which celebrates the end of the Ramzan fast. Muslim enclaves brighten up with new clothes, family visits and merry feasts - which welcome their friends and neighbours of all faiths. Muslim practices here are no different from those of their co-religionists in the region - especially south India.

Pierced for Piety. An old woman fulfils a vow to the god Skanda at Kataragama by piercing his cheeks in penitance.

Facing page: *Cooking sweet rice outside the Hindu temple, to be distributed amongst the devotees as "prasad".*

Gems of Ratnapura

The town of Ratnapura in Sri Lanka owes its name to its abundant resources of invaluable gems, paving the way to fortune for may of its inhabitants and making Sri Lanka the leading source of precious and semi-precious stones. These gems, apart from their obvious ornamental value, have other talismanic properties as well and are highly revered as neutralising agents of evil influences. The therapeutic effects of astral gems are widely publicised, though there are stringent conditions for such usage—for instance, the stone should conform to the exact standards of purity, quality and colour and should be in direct and constant contact with the skin.

While semi-precious stones like amethyst, topaz, garnet, moonstone and agate are astounding in their range of beauty and colour, sapphires, rubies and alexandrite are among the more expensive indigenous gems. Some of these gems have adorned the crowns of Britain and Iran, while the American Natural History Museum displays the unparalleled and largest sapphire in the world, of Sri Lankan origin, weighing 563 carats.

The Lively Arts
---------- ✳ ----------

Dance played no role in the ascetic rituals of Sri Lanka's Theravada Buddhist tradition. However, solemn chants and the music of drums and the flute have always been integrated in formal religious ceremonies and processions. But ancient carvings show men and women in vigorous dance with drums and cymbals. Sadly, we will never know the music they danced to, as the old chronicles of monkish scribes primly carry neither description nor notation of these silent dancers now frozen in stone. In all likelihood the traditions of secular dance gradually declined and disappeared with the fall of the powerful ancient kingdoms, their royal families and noble entourages. But even the kingdoms of the diaspora saw themselves as protectors of Buddhism and patrons of the arts and did all they could do to maintain the art, culture and ceremonials of their glorious forebearers. The last kings of the doomed kingdom of Kandy were isolated from their Asian neighbours by an impenetrable barrier of a European dominated coastline. They could no longer intermingle with the wide reservoir of Asian cultures as their predecessors did. Their 'high' culture became, inevitably, insular and regressed into folk art. However, these kings saw themselves as the protectors of the mystic link between Buddhism and the Sinhala polity. They lavished patronage on all temples and, particularly, the Dalada Maligawa, which enshrined the sacred Tooth Relic of the Buddha. The rituals, ceremonies and processions integral to its worship preserved centuries-old traditions. Finally in 1815, when the nobles of this sad kingdom surrendered their king to the British, they insisted on the preservation and protection of Buddhism and its time-honoured rituals. It is on this account that these Buddhist rituals are yet vital and alive today, as exemplified in the annual glory of the Esala Perahera. The dancers and musicians of the Dalada Maligawa, fostered by traditional families and clans, tied by land and loyalty to the temple have proved to be the fount of modern Sinhala dance and music.

Colonial rule led to an inevitable decline of all traditional art forms. The disappearance of royal patronage to the country arts meant the onset of terminal decay. The emerging elite spurned tradition and adopted the life styles and artistic tastes of Europe. Providentially, religion and tradition were yet preserved at the grass roots. Ancient temples and dependent clans of dancers and musicians kept alive age-old songs and dances integral to the rituals of community worship and folk festivals. The movement for political independence, which began

Facing page: Upekha, the daughter of Sri Lanka's most outstanding dancers, Chitrasena and Vajira, at a performance.

about seventy-five years ago, was accompanied by a burgeoning interest in visible symbols of the national heritage—ancient monuments, national languages, folk costumes, song and dance. Inspired by the cultural revival fostered by Rabindranath Tagore in India, bold pioneers in Sri Lanka went back to their village roots to study traditional songs and dance, at the feet of long-neglected masters of traditional forms.

Ever since independence was achieved in 1948 there has been an explosion in the development of song and dance. This has been accompanied by significant adaptations, as was both inevitable and essential. Mere reproduction of the old ceremonial dances on a modern stage were seen to be repetitive and meaningless when isolated from their traditional context. This realization inspired two developments. The first was the adaptation of traditional steps and rhythms to depict

The beat of drums echoes through the still of the night.

dramatically timeless romances and legends of yore. More recently ballets have been developed to present modern and even revolutionary themes. The second significant development was the emergence of women dancers, who earlier had no role in traditional dance. They adopted the masculine athleticism of the old dance forms to a gentler, more rhythmic, idiom. Today, Sri Lanka has many women dancers, most of them originally trained in schools where dance and music have been firmly integrated into the curriculum. Every village school throbs to the music of drums and the flute. The larger schools all boast of school bands in colourful costumes who lead marches playing traditional airs on drums and flutes of ancient design.

While the main, formal dance forms of the country are based on the rituals of the Kandyan temples, there is yet another vital form of dance in the maritime south. These are the dances of exorcism, popularly known as "devil dances". They are traditionally performed all night to exorcise demons of disease. Dancers in fierce, elaborately carved and fiendish masks prance, somersault and cartwheel to hypnotic drum beats. Their costumes, rhythms and steps are derived from a totally different school of dance. Providing comic relief to these performances are many folk dances of earthy comedy where comically masked figures strut and dance episodes of drunken old men and frisky wives. These dances too have now been absorbed into the repertoire of today's dance ensembles.

Distinctly different are the Carnatic music and Bharata Natyam dances of the Tamil people which are identical to those of Tamil Nadu—their

Rings of fire during a temple procession.

ancestral home. Among dancers, Chitrasena stands as a colossus, as does his wife and prima ballerina, Vajira. Together they pioneered new dance forms, skilfully transcending tradition and resisting the catchy populism of Indian film dances. Parallel with Chitrasena has developed the singer Amaradeva—who stands out among the dancers and who, in many ways, created the modern Sinhala song. All that existed before were either ritual or folk songs. These new singers adapted the old rhythms and formalized their music to sing lyrics of love and longing to a new and enthusiastic audience. Radio and television have given them a tremendous prominence and also developed a wide range of singers catering to the full gamut of tastes from pop to mid-brow to Indo-classical.

There does not seem to have been any tradition of high drama in Sri Lanka. But folk drama has survived where, during the New Year holiday season, village actors perform songs and dance to enact Jataka stories, of the Buddha's previous incarnation, interspersed with skits of topical comedy. The earliest modern plays emerged in the early decades of this century when there were richly costumed verse operettas of heroic and romantic themes from history. For a brief period after this there flourished a few theatrical troupes who wrote their own melodramatic modern plays. These later became the first Sinhala films.

The middle fifties saw a cultural renaissance with the grant of official paramountcy and patronage to the Sinhala language. This inspired a new genre of drama whose defining play was "Maname" written and produced by Saratchandra, a university professor. He had experimented with many

Crimson and Gold. Temple chieftains (Nilames) in the bejewelled traditional costume they adapted from the clothes of 16th century Portuguese hidalgos. They walk in quiet dignity in the annual 'Navam Perahera' procession of Ganga Vihara, in Colombo.

dramatic styles based both on European and Sanskrit models but with limited success. But Maname was an instant and tremendous success. Its theme was an ancient Buddhist tale, the popular subject of a folk play. What raised it to genius was the loveliness of the lyrics sung to music based on folk songs and dances. The introduction of a participatory chorus was a total innovation. Saratchandra wrote more such plays, expressing an increasing complexity of emotion. His success encouraged other

Facing page: *The gloriously robed and illuminated magnificent tusker proudly bears the bejewelled Buddhist reliquary. Escorted by chieftains on attendant elephants, he walks in the Navam Perahera procession of Gangarama Vihara in Colombo.*
Following pages 70-71: *Upekha, the well-known dancer is seen in concert, to honour the 30th Anniversary of her mother's career.*

playwrights too to go back to tradition and there were many interesting plays based on Jataka stories, historical episodes and folk comedies.

The interest in drama which sprang from Saratchandra's impetus yet remains alive. Schools of drama flourish, and plays are written and regularly produced in the major towns. An interesting development has been the political play where thinly veiled satire involving a mythical country is linked to a parallel from legend or history.

Cinema too is very alive and film-stars have become almost cult figures and even political icons. Most films follow the popular South Asian formula of song and dance, violence and villainy, love and romance. However, there has always been a core of good and serious films which have also been popular. These have been generally based on strong scripts originating from stories by notable authors. They have

Larger than Life. Outsize posters of film stars decorate a hoarding in Colombo.

dwelt, with commendable honesty, on themes of social concern—village hypocrisy, social expectation, woman's assertiveness, political fraud and racial hatred. Outstanding directors such as Lester James Pieris, Vasantha Obeysekera, Nihalsingha and Sumithra Peris have achieved international acclaim.

Television has proved to be a fertile field for creative minds and the many TV channels in the country abound with "teledramas". Many of them are serials that run for months and have a popular following. Interestingly many of these dramas depict village life and address contemporary issues.

Facing page: *Partners. A gypsy and his performing monkey.*

Ancient Murals and Traditional Architecture

*

$\mathcal{A}$ll that remains of the art of ancient Sri Lanka are the murals on the walls of old Buddhist temples. Time and weather are rapidly fading the oldest examples to be found at the Tivanka image house at Polonnaruwa where a richly painted vestibule leads up to the towering Buddha of brick. These wall paintings are in panels in a continuous frieze depicting the lives of the Buddha. There is a charming continuity in these friezes where each episode - almost cinematically - merges with the next. They are, in many ways, a time capsule depicting the narrative in the costumes, regalia and domestic background of the artist's own time.

This tradition of temple wall-paintings persisted unbroken for centuries, and is yet alive as is to be seen in the vestibules of every Buddhist Vihara. They are an interesting record of changing life-styles over the centuries. The most famous of the temple paintings of the Kandyan kingdom are those on the walls and ceiling of the Degaldoruwa cave temple. The figures are stylized but lively and composed in well defined groups to tell their sacred story. Temples of the Victorian era in the maritime provinces provide a fascinating window into the life of that era, with fascinating incongruities of courtiers and noble ladies of the Buddha's day dressed in tail coats, cranolines and plumed hats!

Absolutely unique in Sri Lanka's artistic heritage are the frescoes in the rocky alcoves of the mountain palace of Sigiriya. These are the only surviving examples of art for beauty and not for any didactic purpose. Exquisite paintings of noble ladies, in delicate colours waft among painted clouds. They are as fresh today as when they were painted 1,500 years ago. Visitors of many centuries ago were so bewitched they scribbled haunting love poems on the ancient walls of the palace — visible to this day.

Superbly artistic modern temple paintings illumine the interior of Kelaniya temple on the outskirts of Colombo. Little Gotami Vihara tucked away in a rural corner of the city, glows with the magnificent

Facing page: The magnificent Sedent Buddha image sits under a Makara thorana in the 14th century Gadaladeniya temple in Kandy. The temple was built by Buvaneka Bahu IV and is built entirely of stone in the South Indian style.
Following pages 76-77: A deity's effigy at the inner shrine of the Kelaniya Raja Maha Vihara, one of the most sacred Buddhist shrines situated close to Colombo. This site is believed to have been visited by the Buddha over 2500 years ago.

Buddhist murals of George Keyt, the country's greatest modern painter.

Modern art in Sri Lanka is little more than seventy-five years old. Early efforts veered between pallid representational oils and imitations of old frescoes. Fifty or so years ago, around the time the country gained independence, a group of young artists broke away from this straitjacket and began to paint boldly in their own idioms. Foremost among them was George Keyt who painted vigorously even in his nineties. He delved deep into traditional myth and the perennial rhythms of village life to develop the unique style which won him international accolades. These pioneers have inspired a host of interesting painters and a discerning audience.

Although the artistic genius of the monumental Buddhist sculptures of

Frescoes from the Subhodarama temple in Dehiwela, close to the capital.

Anuradhapura and Polonnaruwa was never matched in later ages, it can be said that the consummate skills of ancient craftsmen working in precious metals, pearls, gems and ivory have continued to modern times, though on a lesser scale. Images of the Buddha, Bodhisattvas and gods of exquisite beauty cast in bronze and gold, have recently toured major Western museums in a highly acclaimed exhibition. Recent excavations have unearthed beautifully set jewelery over a thousand years old. Ancient Sri Lanka not only exported the pearls found off Mannar and the gems mined in the foothills of Sri Pada, but also set

Facing page: Legends in Colour. Wall paintings of the Buddha's life drawn as a continuous narrative in panels. These paintings, about 150 years old, depict ancient scenes in Victorian settings with delicious naivety.

them in jewelery of outstanding loveliness and craftsmanship. These traditions were maintained by the last kingdom of Kandy and have been preserved and fostered to this day. Elaborate objects of brass, originally turned out for ceremonial and religious use, have now become collectors' items. Trays, pedestal oil lamps, cutlery and jewel boxes are intricately carved with traditional stylized swans, elephants and lotuses. Traditional women's jewelery continues to be painstakingly made by hereditary craftsmen.

Ivory and tortoiseshell are 'prohibited substances' today in order to protect our dwindling wild life. In ancient times, and till very recently, these exotic materials were major items of foreign trade and the medium for many beautiful objects of devotion and ornamentation. They can yet be seen in temples, museums and homes.

Lankatilleke temple, Kandy—The magnificent Kandyan Lankatilleke temple built in the 14th century by King Buvanekabahu IV, lies castle-like on a rocky hill overlooking lush paddy fields.

Lacquer work has remained almost a monopoly of the Kandyan area. Skilled carpenters turn out trays, ceremonial containers as well as handles for canopies and ornamental spoons whose unique beauty lies in their painstakingly lacquered whorls of red, yellow and black.

Sri Lankan skills in carpentry were recognized hundreds of years ago by the Portuguese and Dutch colonial masters, who used them to turn out domestic furniture from the rich wood of the rich forests. The Dutch in particular struck a responsive chord in the Sinhala carpenter and gave rise to an entire new school of furniture, which adapted Dutch designs of the 18th century to the traditional wood turning and rattan working skills of carpenters. Their antique couches, chairs, tables and beds have become prized collectors' items today. What is interesting, however, is that these designs were so popular that many homes and temples yet possess furniture of these old designs. The current fad has revived the old skills and reproduction of antique furniture has become a thriving industry.

The fall of the Kandyan kingdom had a far-reaching impact on the life-style of its peoples. Traditional hierarchical links that welded peasantry, nobility, clergy and royalty were dissolved. No longer was there a palace with a resident king crowning a society with strictly graded styles of homes and costumes. Over the centuries the isolation of the kingdom led to an almost cosy domestic style of architecture devoid of grandeur. The palace of the last king, situated next to the Dalada Maligawa, saddens one with its stolid simplicity with just a few bas-reliefs to enliven its brick walls. The houses of the nobles were

Moorish Mansion. This lovely old ho... in ...

correspondingly nond... of brick and tile, with small exterior win... ...rtyard.

There is, ho... ...tecture to be found in Buddhist t... ...tic is their stepped steep r... ...brass or terra cotta. Eac... ...ous is the lovely ... Gadaladeniya Vihara ...uth Indian influence. ...ed pillars showing Kandy the steeped ...ng by rocks across ...t region.

In the maritime provinces it was the Dutch who influenced building styles. Many old houses of that period still survive in Colombo's army quarters, though in a sadly run down state. Their main characteristics are wide verandahs supported by chastely carved wooden pillars. This style, on a minor scale, became thoroughly indigenised and can be seen in many houses along the southern roads. The best preserved examples of Dutch architecture are to be found within the intact walls of Galle Fort. Within its narrow streets the centuries-old houses bunched together are interspersed with more impressive government buildings. It is Sri Lanka's nearest approximation to a walled city of medieval Europe.

The little mud walled cottages of peasants, thatched with straw or coconut palms, stand in lush little gardens of jak, breadfruit and mango

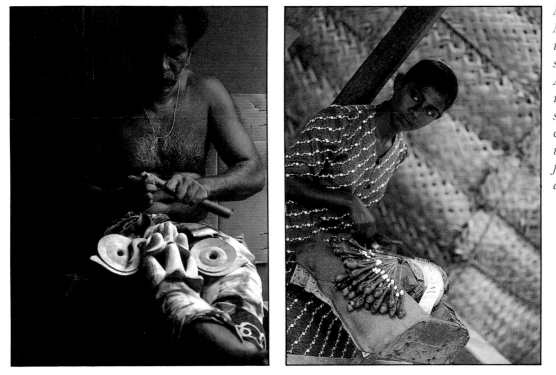

Makers of Masks. Skilled wooden sculptors of Ambalangoda in the south specialise in carving wooden masks for exorcist dancers.

and give the land a lived-in feeling. They are not clustered but scattered amongst paddy fields, coconuts or up distant hills to which they precariously cling. These little homes are a true reflection of the character of the people.

Bustling bazars strung out along main roads are a characteristic feature. They are an almost unbroken series of shop fronts ranging from flamboyant modern shop windows flaunting the latest electronic gadgets to the dark and cool alcoves of ayurvedic pharmacies with the strange

***Facing page:** Humble homes. A typical village scene-a woman fondly holds her baby at the doorway of her humble home of wattle and daub, thatched with coconut palm. These rural houses are a common sight in the remote areas of the country, still unspoilt by the ever increasing industrialisation.*

pungent odours of their stock-in-trade—gnarled roots, dried herbs and berries, and phials of dark and fragrant oils. On their doorsteps squat vendors of betel leaf with their ramshackle racks catering to the people's daily chew, which spatter the gutters blood red. Many bazaars are over a century old and above their tarted up modern facades cling delightfully carved pilasters, balustrades and balconies now sadly crumbling into decay.

The capital of Colombo had been described as a garden city on account of the lavish spread of huge flowering trees in Cinnamon Gardens where the elite live. Age, monsoons and building frenzy have brought down many old trees but many savenues yet remain shaded by gnarled old trees. The city proper is inevitably losing its old character. Impressive, but sadly charactcrless, skyscrapers now tower over a skyline which was earlier crowned only by a light house and clock

Fruits of the Earth. Vegetables displayed for sale in Colombo's market.

tower surrounded by massive neo-classical government buildings and cool shopping arcades of the British era.

An unfettered individuality marks the house-styles of the rich and famous. There is nothing of the understated conformity of the Eurpean townscape. Pseudo-Moghul palaces abut Victorian mansions with towering gates; cold modernist cubes stand next to rustic Kandyan styled mansions bristling with carefully garnered antique artifacts. Modern Sri Lankan architecture may not have a consistent vision but it does make a fascinating melange.

Facing page: *Civic Dignity. Colombo's Roman style Town Hall built by a British Mayor.*

85

Men and Women:
A Nation's Destiny
——— ✳ ———

Sri Lanka's progress towards political independence in 1948 was staid and constitutional. A westernized elite of lawyers and land owners, gradually negotiated for and acquired greater home rule, universal franchise and an elected legislature. Thus when independence dawned, all that remained for Ceylon to acquire was control over its minuscule armed forces and foreign policy. A current of radicalism was, however, always present in the sphere of politics.

Earth Mothers. Women transplanting paddy in the rice fields of Polonnaruwa.

A rising wave of pride in the nation's heritage spearheaded by traditional leaders—monks, village school teachers and physicians—strengthened the hands of politicians who pressed for political independence. At the same time there developed another stream of Marxist radicalism introduced, strangely enough, by young scions of the elite who had acquired their revolutionary ardour while studying in Britain. These young men soon entered the comforting embrace of parliamentary democracy which channelled their skills into debate and compromise. But their most significant contribution was outside the legislature where they pioneered the establishment of powerful

Facing page: *Burden of Bananas. Bunches of bananas bow the sturdy back of a worker at the wholesale market in Colombo's Pettah.*

trade unions in the industrial and plantation sectors. These leaderless workers now became tightly organized, led by the articulate and charismatic young leaders of the Left and emerged as a powerful element in the country's life.

Their strength was consolidated and made visible by strikes called in essential industries and government institutions. There is no doubt that the impetus for Sri Lanka's adoption of worker-friendly welfare policies, unique in the South Asian region, was the radicalism of these pioneers who, later, rose to Cabinet rank acquiring the power to implement the policies they had agitated for.

This peaceful political progress was brutally interrupted in 1971 by a totally unexpected armed uprising. A charismatic revolutionary skilfully orchestrated the bitter dissatisfaction of rural Sinhala youth deprived of

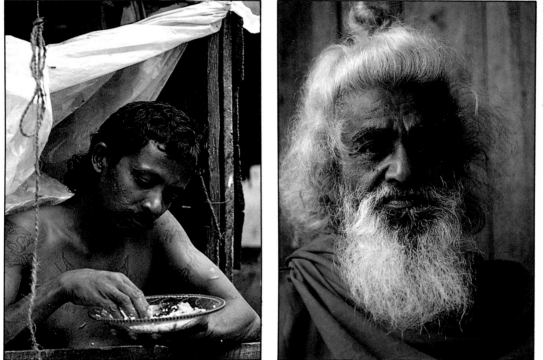

Left. *A labourer enjoying his meal of curry and rice.*

Right. *A devotee with knotted hair in Kataragama.*

opportunities that, they felt, their education entitled them to. The uprising was defeated by the government within a month or two. Its leaders were brought to trial and jailed. But this bloody uprising traumatised the body politic and rural Sinhala society lost its innocence.

Almost a decade later Tamil youth led by another charismatic figure launched another uprising protesting against perceived inequities in the treatment of the Tamil community. This rebellion received covert overseas aid and developed into a demand for a separate Tamil state. This is not a demand that the government will ever accede to. As a result the national security forces and the Tamil rebels have been locked

Facing page: *Saffron and yellow-robed nuns relax outside a temple wall, awaiting the Buddhist sermon to commence.*

in combat for many years, causing considerable loss of life. Meanwhile the government continues to negotiate with the moderate Tamil parties in Parliament to grant greater regional autonomy to Tamil majority areas. Ironically most Tamils in the country live and work peacefully, and play significant roles in the country's government and political life.

The Sinhala women of Sri Lanka have often played a significant role, because traditionally they have enjoyed an independent status. Their independent status has been enshrined in Buddhism and customary law. The major reason for this phenomenon, unique in the South Asian region, has been the equal status granted to women in Buddhism. It is the only major religion that absorbed women into the clergy. Chronicles record that thousands of women took to the monastic life inspired by the nun Sanghamitta who carried the sacred Bo-sapling to Sri Lanka

Stone Washed. A rural washer woman beats dirty linen clean on a rock in a lotus pond.

2,300 years ago. It is also recorded that these intrepid nuns sailed as missionaries to far-off China to establish the order of nuns that yet continues as a viable community. The vicissitudes of history—invasion, famine, disease and foreign conquest - sadly led to the demise of the order of Buddhist nuns in Sri Lanka. The independence of spirit shown by these pious women obviously was in keeping with Sinhala tradition as is exemplified in the recorded laws of the Kandyan kingdom, which are yet legally valid. Sinhala women today retain their personal names

Facing page: *Bath of Purification. Pilgrims travelling to the shrine of the God Skanda at Kataragama in the south-eastern part of the country, take a ritual bath in the Menik Ganga (River of Gems) before they cross it to pray for boons*
Following pages 92-93: *Sea and the City. A family paddles in the sea at Colombo's marine esplanade, Galle Face Green.*

even after marriage and control their own property. They have equal rights when it comes to obtaining a divorce. There also exists the 'binna' form of marriage where a woman who has no brothers, marries a consort who takes her family name and passes it on to their children. Anchored in this tradition of independence, Sri Lanka has been led by many queens in ancient times. Legendary among them was Queen Anula, not for her achievements but for her vigorous love life!

Women in colonial Ceylon won voting rights at the same time as men in 1932. Since then there have always been women elevated to the national legislature as well as local authorities. The first woman minister was appointed to the Cabinet in 1956 and since then there have always been women ministers in every government. Sri Lanka earned its place in the history of women's achievements when Mrs. Sirimavo Bandaranaike became the world's first woman Prime Minister. This was a position she held with distinction more than once and for many years. Recently her daughter Mrs. Chandrika Bandaranaike Kumaratunga, after brief spells as a Provincial Chief Minister and Prime Minister, was elevated to the post of Executive President at a national election. Women in Sri Lanka's politics now play a key role in determining the country's destiny.

Educational opportunities for girls have been identical with those for boys. As a result women's literacy is also almost 90% and a record for a less developed country. This literacy has meant that there is a considerable increase in the percentage of women employed in all walks of life. In the teaching and medical professions they outnumber men. This has deeper implications. Women tend to marry late, in their mid-twenties, and have smaller families. And their life expectancy of over 75 outstrips that of men. A very recent socio-economic phenomenon has been triggered by the comparative absence of taboos on Sri Lankan women pursuing a career away from home. This phenomenon has been the tremendous outflow of women for domestic service in oil rich Arab countries. What began as a trickle has now become a flood, and the government has stepped in to monitor the process of outflow and the welfare of these courageous women who have left to seek their fortune. The inward remittances of these women now constitute one of the major sources of foreign exchange earned by the country. There is no doubt that these humble women are endowed with the same qualities of independence, self-esteem and courage as the nuns and queens of ancient times and the professionals, prime ministers and presidents of today.

Sri Lanka's many attractions have always drawn visitors to its shores since ancient times when Marco Polo and Ibn Batuta came this way following the silk road of the sea. But tourism, in the modern sense, has been a phenomenon of the last three decades or so when the state and private sector entrepreneurs embarked on a promotional programme. The lovely beaches of the south-west, ranging from the five-star to simple cabanas for the back-packer, the hills surrounding Kandy, the former colonial hill resort of Nuwara Eliya nestling amidst tea plantations and fir trees, and the ancient cities of Anuradhapura, Polonnaruwa and Sigiriya are just some of the sites to explore.

The sheer variety of the country is of great appeal. It is far more than a sunny beach with multiple back ups. A short walk will immerse the traveller in the vibrant life around him—a procession, a fish auction, worshippers at an old temple, folk weavers of lace and handlooms, a dance of exorcism. In Kandy one can yet see the vestiges of the last kingdom in the nightly rituals of the Dalada Maligawa, and the carved pillars and painted walls of lesser known temples nestling amidst terraced fields. Anuradhapura, Polonnaruwa and Sigiriya overwhelm one with the massive scale of their stone sculptures, ruined monasteries and

Shop in the Jungle. A little wayside stall by a forested road selling king-coconuts to the thirsty traveller.

vast reservoirs. The hill country is a different story - sinuous roads through hills and mountains covered with a blanket of tea bushes; a fragrant whiff of tea as one passes tea factories, rock rhododendrons, firs, eucalyptus and mist. Last of all, the rich wilderness of the great national parks of Yala in the south-east are home to deer, elephant, leopard, wild boar. To its marshes every year fly migrant flamingoes, snipe and duck from Arctic Siberia.

Above all Sri Lanka is a lovely and hospitable land and its people are imbued with the gentle friendliness that comes from millennia of civilized life in a land to which Nature has been more than kind.

Following page 96: *The age of innocence.*

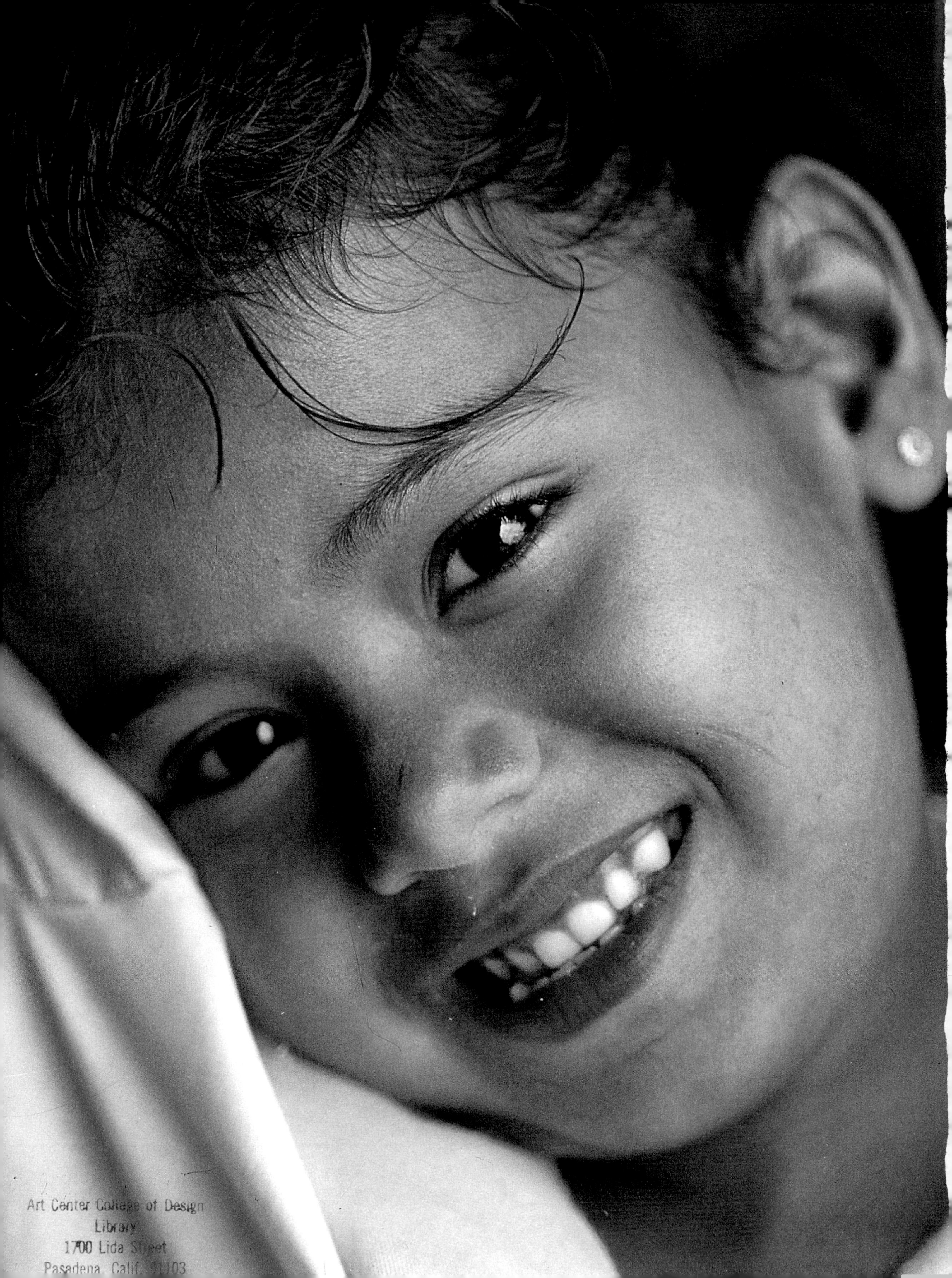